26"

Handling
Cancer

by Carla Mooney

Content Consultant

Christopher Donnelly, DDS, PhD
Postdoctoral Fellow
Duke University

Handling
Health Challenges

Essential Library
An Imprint of Abdo Publishing
abdobooks.com

abdobooks.com

Published by Abdo Publishing, a division of ABDO, PO Box 398166, Minneapolis, Minnesota 55439. Copyright © 2022 by Abdo Consulting Group, Inc. International copyrights reserved in all countries. No part of this book may be reproduced in any form without written permission from the publisher. Essential Library™ is a trademark and logo of Abdo Publishing.

Printed in the United States of America, North Mankato, Minnesota.
052021
092021

Cover Photo: iStockphoto
Interior Photos: Katarzyna Bialasiewicz/iStockphoto, 4, 58–59; JHVE Photo/iStockphoto, 7; Shutterstock Images, 10, 24, 36, 51, 55, 65, 78; Drima Film/Shutterstock Images, 14; Douglas Olivares/iStockphoto, 18; iStockphoto, 26, 33; Tyler Olson/Shutterstock Images, 29; Dr P. Marazzi/Science Source, 39; Mark Kostich/Shutterstock Images, 42; Mstudio Images/iStockphoto, 48; Dragon Images/iStockphoto, 61; FatCamera/iStockphoto, 70; Jon Shapley/Houston Chronicle/AP Images, 73; Alexander Image/Shutterstock Images, 81; Karel Noppe/Shutterstock Images, 87; Elaine Thompson/AP Images, 88; Amber Arnold/Wisconsin State Journal/AP Images, 92; Keith Chambers/Science Source, 94; David Parry/PA Wire/URN:37088733/Press Association/AP Images, 98

Editor: Arnold Ringstad
Series Designer: Megan Ellis

Library of Congress Control Number: 2020948031

Publisher's Cataloging-in-Publication Data

Names: Mooney, Carla, author.   DEC 0 1 2021
Title: Handling cancer / by Carla Mooney
Description: Minneapolis, Minnesota : Abdo Publishing, 2022 | Series: Handling health challenges | Includes online resources and index.
Identifiers: ISBN 9781532194955 (lib. bdg.) | ISBN 9781098215262 (ebook)
Subjects: LCSH: Cancer--Juvenile literature. | Carcinogens--Juvenile literature. | Cocarcinogens--Juvenile literature. | Cancer--Social aspects--Juvenile literature. | Therapeutics--Juvenile literature. | Health--Juvenile literature.
Classification: DDC 616.994--dc23

Contents

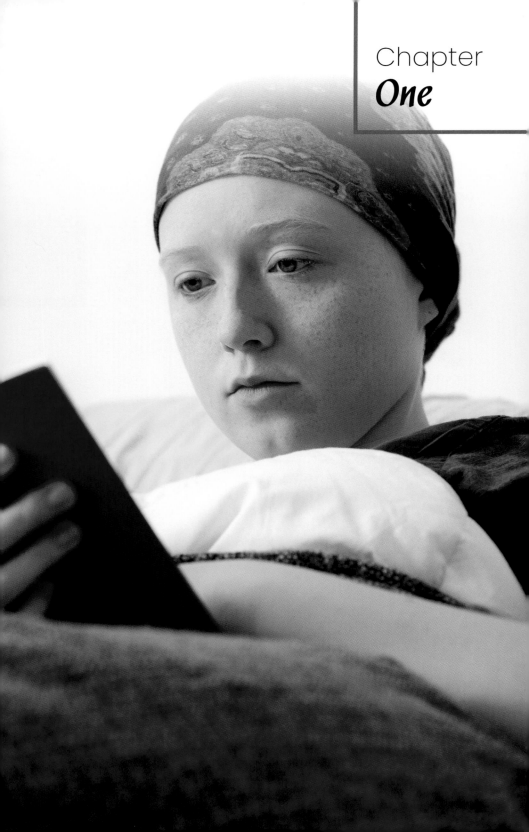

Living with Cancer

It's Monday morning, and Aidan has an appointment in the oncology clinic at ten. He gets out of bed and pulls on a T-shirt, sweatpants, and sneakers. Clinic appointments can last a long time, and he wants to be comfortable.

Aidan rubs a generous amount of lidocaine cream over a small bump on his upper chest to numb the skin. The bump is his port, a small device that has been surgically placed under the skin of his chest. It connects to a blood vessel. His medical team uses it to give him fluids, blood transfusions, and anticancer drug treatments known as chemotherapy. They can even draw blood for testing from his port. Today, a nurse will use it to draw blood and administer chemotherapy. Since Aidan got the port, he no longer

> Cancer is relatively rare among teens, but for those who have it, it can create considerable challenges.

Receiving Chemotherapy through a Port

When a person has cancer, he or she usually has to receive a lot of intravenous (IV) medications, fluids, and sometimes blood transfusions. To make it easier to handle these IV needs over a long period, many people have a port placed. A port is a small disc about the size of a quarter that is made of plastic or metal. During a short outpatient surgery, doctors place a port just under the skin, usually on a person's chest. A soft, thin tube connects the port directly to a large vein. Nurses can administer chemotherapy medicines to a patient using a special needle that fits into the port. They can also draw blood through the port. When a patient has finished chemotherapy treatment, the port is removed through another outpatient surgery.

has to sit through repeated needle pokes to find a vein in his arm.

He's not being sedated today for a spinal tap, a procedure that involves removing spinal fluid for testing and administering chemotherapy. That means Aidan can eat breakfast before he leaves for the hospital. His mother makes his favorite omelet—ham and cheese—with a side of buttered toast. After breakfast, Aidan tosses his favorite baseball cap on his head. His hair is just starting to grow back, and it feels downy soft. He and his mother get into the car and drive downtown to the clinic.

At the Clinic

When they arrive, they check in at the front desk and wait to be called back to an examination room by the nurses. When it is Aidan's turn, the nurse takes his weight, temperature, and blood pressure. Then, she

Cancer clinics have the experts and equipment needed for modern cancer treatments.

Acute Lymphoblastic Leukemia

Acute lymphoblastic leukemia (ALL) is a type of blood cancer. It starts in the white blood cells inside the bone marrow, which is the soft inner part of the bone where blood cells are made. White blood cells fight infection and protect the body from disease. In a person with ALL, the bone marrow produces immature cells that develop into abnormal white blood cells called lymphoblasts. The abnormal lymphoblasts do not function properly. The cells build up in the bone marrow and blood, and they begin to crowd out healthy blood cells. Without enough normal white blood cells, the body has a hard time fighting infections. ALL is the most common type of cancer in children. Approximately 3,000 people under age 20 are diagnosed with ALL each year in the United States.[1] It is considered a highly treatable form of cancer, and with proper medical care, most people can expect to get better.

accesses his port and draws some blood to send to the lab for testing. Every time Aidan comes to the clinic, the oncology lab tests his blood, checking his red and white blood cell counts and platelet levels. Doctors also look to make sure the leukemia cells, called blasts, have not returned.

Today the doctor brings good news: Aidan's blood counts look good and his blood is still clear of leukemia cells. She examines Aidan. She talks to him and his mother about how he is feeling and asks about any side effects he may be experiencing. The doctor explains that the leg weakness he feels is a normal side effect of one of his chemotherapy drugs. If it becomes more of a problem and interferes with his walking, she can prescribe some physical therapy for him.

When Aidan was first diagnosed with acute lymphoblastic leukemia (ALL), he spent a lot of time in the hospital and had weekly clinic visits. Now that he's more than a year into his three-plus years of treatment, he only has to come to the clinic once a month for blood tests and intravenous (IV) chemotherapy. The rest of the time, he takes medication at home to keep the leukemia at bay.

When today's appointment is finished, Aidan and his mother stop at the hospital cafeteria for a bag of popcorn. It's a tradition they started when he first began cancer treatment and one that he looks forward to each time they come to the hospital. Then, they head home. Aidan will be back next month.

> "When cancer is caught early, there is usually a good treatment for it. I would advise them not to give in—just hang in there."[2]
>
> —Jason, a patient with chronic myelogenous leukemia

Support from family and friends can help a person with cancer remain positive and upbeat.

Every Cancer Experience Is Unique

Most people know someone who is living with cancer. In 2019 there were approximately 1.8 million new cases of cancer diagnosed.[3] Many of these patients were diagnosed with breast cancer, the most common cancer diagnosis. Other common types include lung, prostate, colon, bone, brain, and skin cancers.

Each person who has cancer will have a unique experience. There is no typical or average cancer journey. That's because every case of cancer is different on a molecular level. Cancer is not a single disease. It is a wide variety of diseases, all of which involve an abnormal growth of cells in the body. These cells originally come from the person's own cells, but they have mutated, or changed, and they no longer function the way they should. Two people with the same type of cancer can have different symptoms

Racial and Ethnic Divide

According to a 2019 report from the American Cancer Society, the rates of new cancer cases and cancer-related deaths vary by race and ethnic group. In 2016 the cancer death rate was 14 percent higher in Black Americans as compared to whites.[4] Asian Americans had the lowest rates of new cancer cases and cancer deaths. These differences by race and ethnic group are related to several factors linked to socioeconomic status. People living in the poorest regions are more likely to smoke and be obese, which are two risk factors for cancer. One contributor to obesity is a concept known as food deserts. Food deserts are urban areas in which it is difficult to find food that is both nutritious and affordable, even as unhealthy food is cheap and plentiful. Poverty also affects how often people can afford to go to the doctor, leading to fewer routine cancer screenings, cancers being diagnosed at later stages, and a lower chance of getting the best treatments. A history of racial bias in the health-care system against Black people is also a factor, since it can lead to distrust of doctors.

and different outcomes. A person's experience with cancer is also affected by his or her environment, the availability of a support system, past experiences, the medical team, treatment side effects, and more.

There is no right or wrong way to feel about living with cancer. It is simply unique for every person.

A person's journey with cancer can change day by day. Sometimes it can even vary by the hour or minute. At one point, a person may feel physically strong, while a few hours later he is struggling with nausea and weakness from the day's chemotherapy treatment. A patient may also experience a roller coaster of emotions. One day she may be joyful after receiving good results on lab tests. The next day, when scans are not as positive, sadness may overcome her. Some days may flow smoothly, while on other days it may feel like every task is an insurmountable hurdle.

Cancer is a serious diagnosis. The disease and its treatments can cause short-term and long-term side

> "Being positive is a big deal. It sounds cliché, but look at the small things in life and enjoy them."[5]
>
> —Victor, a patient living with both chronic lymphocytic leukemia (CLL) and small lymphocytic lymphoma (SLL)

What Is Remission?

When a person undergoes cancer treatment, the goal is remission. Remission is when the signs and symptoms of cancer have lessened or gone away. In partial remission, the cancer is still there, but it is diminished. That might mean that a tumor has shrunk, or in the case of blood cancers, that there are fewer cancer cells in the body. Complete remission occurs when blood tests, physical exams, and imaging scans show no signs of cancer. Complete remission is also called no evidence of disease (NED). Often, patients still need treatment when they are in remission. Treatment reduces the risk of cancer returning in case there are a few cancer cells, which are microscopic in size and may escape detection, remaining in the body. Because cancer can come back, doctors and patients typically avoid using the word *cured* when talking about remission.

effects, and it can be fatal. In 2019 approximately 607,000 people died from cancer in the United States.[6] For people under the age of 65, cancer was the leading cause of death. However, with the right treatment and lifestyle choices, many people living with cancer are able to lead happy and productive lives.

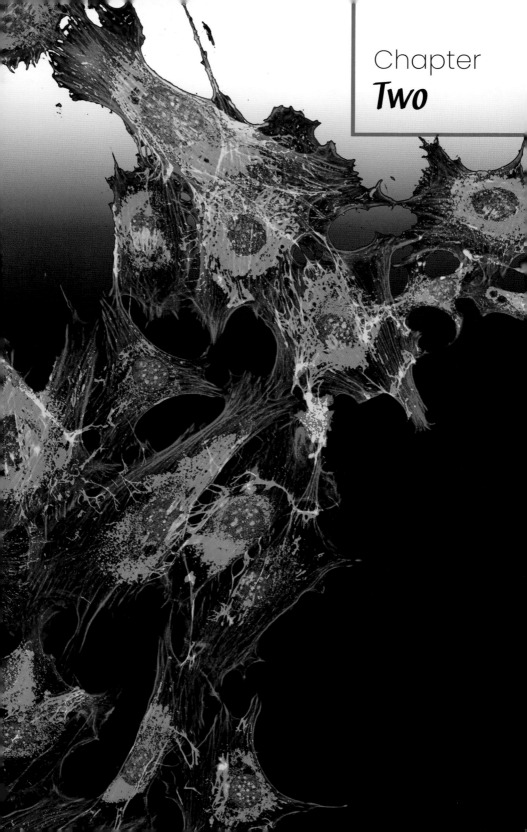

Chapter
Two

What Is Cancer?

Cancer is a collection of related diseases. At the root of all types of cancer is a problem in which certain cells in the body start to grow out of control. The cells multiply without stopping and spread into the healthy tissues and organs nearby.

A Problem with Cells

The human body is made up of trillions of cells, each of which has its own function. The body has skin cells, liver cells, blood cells, brain cells, muscle cells, and more. Normally, healthy cells grow and divide to form new cells as needed. When body cells die, they are replaced by new cells.

When a person has cancer, permanent changes called mutations have occurred in the genetic code of the cancer cells. The normal process of cell division

The common link between all forms of cancer is cells that multiply too fast, negatively affecting the body.

goes off course. Abnormal cells begin to divide and form new cells even when they are not needed. The cell division continues without stopping. The abnormal cells begin to crowd surrounding tissues and impact the normal functioning of the body.

In many types of cancer, the abnormally dividing cells form a solid mass of tissue called a tumor. A cancer tumor is malignant, which means that it can metastasize, or spread into and affect nearby tissues. As malignant tumors grow, some of the abnormal cells can break off from the tumor and travel through the lymphatic system to other parts of the body. From there, the abnormal cancer cells can form new tumors.

Cancer cells are less specialized than healthy cells. Healthy body cells develop into specific cell

What Is Metastasis?

Metastasis occurs when cancer spreads from its initial tumor site to a different body part. Cancer cells from the main tumor break away and enter the blood or lymphatic system. These systems carry the cancer cells throughout the body. When the cells settle, they form new tumors in a different part of the body. The cancer has metastasized. When a cancer spreads to another part of the body, it still has the same name as the original cancer and the same treatment. For example, a lung cancer that spreads to the bones is called metastatic lung cancer, not bone cancer.

types with distinct functions. For example, a brain cell is very different from a skin cell. Each has its own purpose and role in the body's functioning. Cancer cells never mature into distinct cell types. They do not respond to the signals that normally tell cells when to stop dividing, and instead they keep dividing over and over again.

Cancer cells are also able to use the body's healthy cells to grow and stay alive. They can influence surrounding normal cells to form blood vessels that remove waste products and provide tumors with oxygen and nutrients, which they need to grow. Although the body's immune system typically removes damaged cells from the body, similarly to

Lymphatic System

The lymphatic system is a group of organs and tissues that work together to rid the body of waste, toxins, and other unwanted substances. The lymphatic system transports lymph, which is a fluid that carries white blood cells that fight infection, throughout the body. The lymphatic system includes vessels that carry lymph to the lymph nodes. There are hundreds of lymph nodes throughout the body. Some are deep inside the body, while others are closer to the surface. The lymph nodes filter lymph and catch any debris or cells found in the lymph. The lymph nodes also produce and store cells that fight infection and disease. The thymus, spleen, tonsils, and adenoids are also part of the lymphatic system.

how it attacks bacteria and viruses, some cancer cells are able to hide from the immune system.

Types of Cancer

Cancer can develop in any part of the body. As a result, there are more than 100 specific types of cancer. Each type is typically named for the organ or tissue where the cancer forms. For example, breast cancer starts in the cells of breast tissues and skin cancer starts in skin cells. Some types of cancer are more common than others.

Carcinomas are the most common group of cancers. Carcinomas form when epithelial cells,

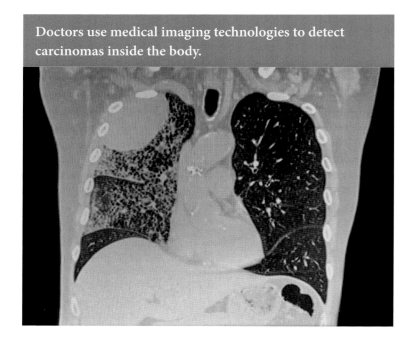

Doctors use medical imaging technologies to detect carcinomas inside the body.

which cover surfaces inside and outside the body such as the skin and the outermost layer of organs, begin to divide out of control. Different kinds of carcinomas develop in different epithelial cells. For example, adenocarcinoma forms in epithelial cells that produce fluids or mucus. They are often found in glandular tissues, though they can also occur in nonglandular tissues, such as the lungs. Most cancers in the breast, colon, and prostate are adenocarcinomas. Basal cell carcinoma forms in the outer layer of a person's skin, while squamous cell carcinoma forms in squamous cells, which lie just beneath the skin's outer surface. Squamous cells also line many organs, such as the stomach, intestines, lungs, bladder, and kidneys. Transitional cell carcinomas form in transitional epithelium tissue, which is found in the linings of the bladder, ureters, and part of the kidneys. Some cancers of these organs are transitional cell carcinomas.

Sarcomas are cancers that form in bone or in some of the body's soft tissues. These tissues include muscle, fat, blood vessels, lymph vessels, tendons, and ligaments. The most common type of sarcoma is osteosarcoma, a cancer of the bone.

Some cancers begin in the bone marrow, where the body produces blood cells. These cancers, called

Brain and Spinal Cord Tumors

Sometimes, tumors form in the brain or on the spinal cord. These tumors, which can be benign or malignant, are abnormal growths of tissue inside the skull or in the spinal column. Both the brain and spinal cord are part of the body's central nervous system (CNS). Because the CNS is enclosed in the hard bone of the skull and spinal column, any abnormal tissue growth can put pressure on sensitive tissue and cause problems. CNS tumors can be caused by certain genetic diseases or by exposure to cancer-causing chemicals or radiation.

leukemias, do not form solid tumors. Instead, abnormal white blood cells build up in the blood and bone marrow. They crowd out healthy blood cells, which makes it difficult for the body to provide oxygen to its tissues, control bleeding, or fight infections. Leukemias are classified according to what type of blood cell the cancer started in and how quickly the cancer cells spread.

Another group of cancers, called lymphomas, begin in the body's lymphocytes. These cells, called T cells and B cells, are white blood cells that function as part of the body's immune system. When a person has lymphoma, abnormal lymphocytes divide and build up in the lymph nodes and other body organs. There are two main types of lymphoma: Hodgkin's lymphoma and non-Hodgkin's lymphoma.

Melanoma is a type of cancer that affects the specialized skin cells that make melanin, which is the pigment that gives skin color. Most melanomas begin on the skin. However, some can form in other tissue that has pigment, such as the eye.

What Causes Cancer?

Cancer is a complex group of diseases, and there are several factors that influence whether a person develops cancer. All types of cancer are caused by a mutation in a person's genes that control how the cells grow, divide, and function. Genes carry the body's instructions for life. They tell cells how to make molecules called proteins. Proteins carry out a variety of essential functions so that the body can survive and grow. Errors in genetic instructions can cause a cell to stop behaving normally and become cancerous.

Benign Tumors

Some tumors are not cancerous. These tumors, called benign tumors, do not spread into nearby tissues as cancerous, malignant tumors do. However, benign tumors can grow to be very large. In some cases, they may grow enough to interfere with the functioning of an organ or nearby tissue. When this happens, doctors will perform surgery to remove the tumor from the body. While most benign tumors are not life-threatening, those that grow in the brain can be very serious and can sometimes be fatal.

Gene mutations have a variety of causes. Some gene mutations are hereditary, or passed from parent to child. Other gene mutations occur after birth and are caused by environmental sources. Smoking, radiation, viruses, hormones, chronic inflammation, a lack of exercise, and exposure to certain cancer-causing chemicals have all been linked to genetic changes that lead to cancer.

In many cases, a single gene mutation does not cause cancer. Instead, scientists believe that a combination of several genetic changes, both inherited and environmental, may work together and cause cancer. For example, people may inherit genetic mutations from their parents that make them more likely to develop cancer, but that does not mean they will definitely develop the disease. Instead, one or more additional gene mutations must occur for cancer to begin. Environmental factors may increase their chances of getting cancer.

Risk Factors

While scientists cannot predict who will get cancer with certainty, several risk factors are known to increase a person's risk of developing it. People with weakened immune systems have a heightened risk. Because some cancers take years to develop, another risk factor is age. People over age 65 are more likely to be diagnosed with cancer than younger people. Chronic health conditions that cause stress to the body's cells, such as obesity or the inflammatory bowel disease ulcerative colitis, can also increase cancer risk.

Lifestyle choices can increase a person's risk of cancer. People who smoke are more likely to develop cancer than nonsmokers. People who drink more than one to two alcoholic drinks daily also have an increased risk of cancer. Frequent exposure to the sun or numerous blistering sunburns increase the risk of cancer. Practicing unsafe sex can also increase the risk of certain cancers.

"We know that cancer does not care about your background. You can be poor or rich, come from a small or large family, and the list goes on."[1]

—*Christina, a breast cancer patient*

Family history is another risk factor for cancer. In some people, an abnormal gene that can lead to cancer is passed from parent to child. Although the abnormal gene itself typically does not cause cancer, it can increase a person's risk of developing the disease. Only about 5 to 10 percent of all cancers result directly from gene mutations inherited from a parent, according to the American Cancer Society.[2]

Exposure to harmful chemicals can also increase the risk of cancer. Secondhand smoke has long been linked to a heightened risk. Certain chemicals in the home or at work, such as asbestos and benzene, can also raise a person's chances of developing cancer.

Preventing Cancer

There is no guaranteed way to prevent cancer. However, scientists have identified several ways to lower a person's risk of developing cancer. Drinking alcohol in moderation, not smoking, and avoiding harmful ultraviolet rays from the sun can all reduce

Workers who remove asbestos from buildings must wear protective gear to avoid exposure.

the risk. In addition, leading a healthy lifestyle by eating a nutritious diet and getting regular exercise can also reduce a person's risk of cancer. Doctors also recommend getting certain immunizations to prevent viral illnesses that increase the risk of certain cancers. These include the hepatitis B and human papillomavirus (HPV) vaccines. The HPV vaccine, which can help prevent cervical cancer as well as some types of throat cancer, has been a major success story in particular. People may also want to schedule cancer screening exams based on their personal risk factors.

Cancer is a serious disease that can strike anywhere in the body. Because of how dangerous it is, cancer is the subject of intense study. Doctors are learning more all the time about how to diagnose and treat each different type of cancer.

"The evidence supporting the use of exercise for cancer prevention and survivorship has grown tremendously in the past decade."[3]

—Linda Trinh, assistant professor at the University of Toronto and specialist in exercise and cancer survivorship, in 2019

Diagnosing Cancer

Cancer can cause a variety of symptoms. A person may experience pain, fever, unexplained weight loss, headaches, lethargy, or just a general feeling of being unwell. Other potential symptoms of cancer are unexplained lumps, changes in bowel or bladder habits, coughs or trouble breathing, unexplained numbness or tingling, and unexplained bleeding or bruising. Because many of these symptoms are often caused by other illnesses or injuries, a person may not think he or she has cancer at first. However, if the symptoms do not go away within a few weeks, a person should see a doctor so he or she can be examined. The earlier cancer is found, the better chance a person has to fully recover.

Many of cancer's symptoms are also caused by other illnesses, so people must visit a doctor to determine what is really wrong, rather than trying to diagnose themselves.

Cancer Screening Tests

Early detection of cancer can save lives. For this reason, scientists recommend cancer screening tests that can detect certain cancers very early in their progression. Some people have a strong family history of certain types of cancer, meaning they have several relatives diagnosed with the same type of cancer. For these people, doctors typically recommend regular screening tests for that type of cancer. In addition, doctors also recommend most adults get routine screening tests for certain cancers regardless of their family history. Routine screening is recommended for skin cancer, head and neck cancer, breast cancer, colorectal cancer, prostate cancer, cervical cancer, and lung cancer. A person's age and other risk factors determine when these screenings should occur.

Diagnosis and Testing

To start, the doctor will perform a physical exam. During the exam, the doctor will examine any lumps. She or he will also look for abnormalities that may indicate a potential cancer, such as changes in skin color, swelling, or the enlargement of an organ. The doctor will also talk to a person about the symptoms and ask the person to describe what he or she is experiencing and feeling. The doctor will probably also order laboratory tests, such as blood and urine tests, to identify any abnormalities that could be a sign of cancer. For example, a blood test can reveal an unusual number of white blood cells in a person with leukemia.

Imaging tests may also be used to diagnose certain types of cancer. Imaging tools such as computerized tomography (CT), magnetic resonance imaging (MRI), positron emission tomography (PET), ultrasounds, and X-rays allow doctors to look inside the body and examine the bones and internal organs without surgery. These imaging tests may reveal

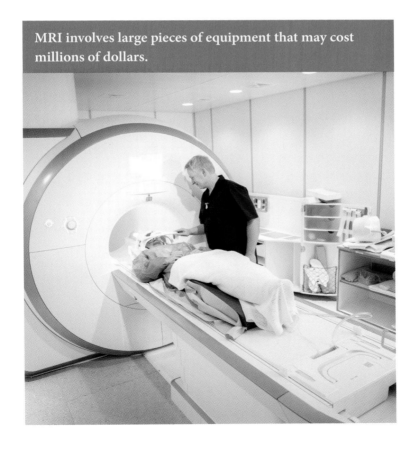

MRI involves large pieces of equipment that may cost millions of dollars.

tumors within the body that are not visible from the outside. Some of these tests, such as X-rays, are fast tests. Others, such as MRI, may require the patient to lie still for a long time while the machine takes the image.

When a doctor identifies a potentially cancerous lump, she may perform a biopsy to collect a sample of cells for laboratory testing. Biopsies can be conducted in several ways, depending on the location and type of mass. In the lab, doctors examine the cell samples under a microscope to identify cancerous cells. With this information, the doctor can diagnose the patient with a specific type of cancer.

A patient, who used the pseudonym Jason when interviewed about his experience, recalled what his

Needle Biopsy

Sometimes doctors will perform a needle biopsy to get more information about a tumor. A needle biopsy is a procedure that gathers a sample of cells from the body that can be sent to a lab for testing. Two types of needle biopsy procedure are fine-needle aspiration and core needle biopsy. In a fine-needle aspiration, the doctor will use a thin, hollow needle and guide it through the skin and into the targeted area. The doctor will draw cells from the area through the needle. The process can be repeated several times until the doctor has collected enough cells. In a core needle biopsy, the doctor uses a wider needle to extract a larger cylinder-shaped piece of tissue to be tested.

cancer diagnosis was like. Jason is an adult male. He was diagnosed with chronic myelogenous leukemia after going to the doctor for abdominal pain. "The doctor thought that the pain was probably caused by some inflammation," he said. Jason continued:

> I was due for some blood work to check my cholesterol level anyway, so they took a blood sample. When the tests for the blood work came back, my white blood cell count was high. I went back a few weeks later to have more blood work done. At that time, my white blood cell count was 136,000 (normal levels are between 4,100 and 10,900). . . . When the doctor got the results from my second round of blood work, he called me into the office and told me I had chronic myelogenous leukemia. I was shocked and scared. I was by myself, so I called my roommate. I just needed to be with someone.[1]

Stages of Cancer

Most cancers are categorized in stages 0 through IV. Generally, the higher the stage, the more advanced the cancer has become. Cancers are considered stage 0 if abnormal cells are found but those cells have not spread to nearby tissue. These abnormal cells have not become full cancer cells yet, but they have the potential to become cancerous in the future. In stages I, II, and III, there are full cancerous cells present. The larger the tumor and the more it has spread into nearby tissue, the higher stage it will be. When cancer reaches stage IV, it has spread to other parts of the body.

Once a person has been diagnosed with cancer, doctors will figure out what stage the cancer has reached. The person may undergo more imaging tests and other procedures to learn the stage and see whether the cancer has spread to other parts of the body. Knowing the stage of cancer can help doctors

Tumor Markers

Tumor markers are things produced by or present in cancer cells that provide information about a cancer. Tumor markers are often proteins or other substances made by cancer cells. There are two main types of tumor markers that are useful during cancer treatment: circulating tumor markers and tissue tumor markers. Circulating tumor markers are found in the patient's blood, stool, urine, and other body fluids. Doctors use these markers to determine a patient's prognosis, detect any remaining or returning cancer after treatment, assess a patient's response to treatment, and monitor whether cancer has become resistant to treatment. Tissue tumor markers are often found when taking a sample of a patient's tumor. These markers are used to diagnose and classify the patient's cancer. Doctors also use tissue tumor markers to estimate a patient's prognosis and select a treatment.

decide on the best treatment plan and determine whether the patient is eligible to participate in any clinical trials. It can also help doctors give a patient an accurate idea of his or her prognosis.

Understanding Prognosis

Once a person finds out he or she has cancer, one of the first questions is often about the prognosis. Many

Hearing about a cancer diagnosis and prognosis can be difficult for patients.

factors affect a patient's prognosis. These include the type of cancer and where it is located in the body. The stage of the cancer and whether it has spread to other parts of the body are additional factors. The cancer's grade, which is a measure of how abnormal the cancer cells look under a microscope, can also affect prognosis. Other factors, such as the person's age and how healthy the person was before getting cancer, can impact how that patient handles the disease and its treatment.

"Hearing the word cancer changed my life in every way imaginable. There suddenly became only one focus, staying alive."[2]

—Ian, a patient diagnosed with T-cell ALL

For some people, understanding their prognosis makes it easier for them to cope with their diagnosis. They may want to ask their doctor about statistics and more information about their cancer. Seeking information about prognosis is a personal decision.

Getting a Second Opinion

When faced with a cancer diagnosis, many patients choose to get a second opinion from a different doctor. Getting a second opinion may help the patient gather more information about the cancer and potential treatment options. The patient may want to find another doctor to examine test results, talk to him or her, and explore different ideas. Talking to another doctor can help patients feel more informed about their diagnosis and more certain of the treatment plan they decide to follow.

"Being diagnosed with cancer is a funny thing. You are welcomed into a unique club with an absolutely brutal initiation ceremony, including but not limited to invasive surgeries, targeted radiation, or poison injected directly into your veins."[3]

—*Brianna Barratt, a patient diagnosed with cancer*

Often a patient's current doctor can recommend another doctor who specializes in the patient's type of cancer to provide a second opinion. Patients can also inquire at local hospitals, cancer centers, or national organizations to find a doctor who has experience with their type of cancer.

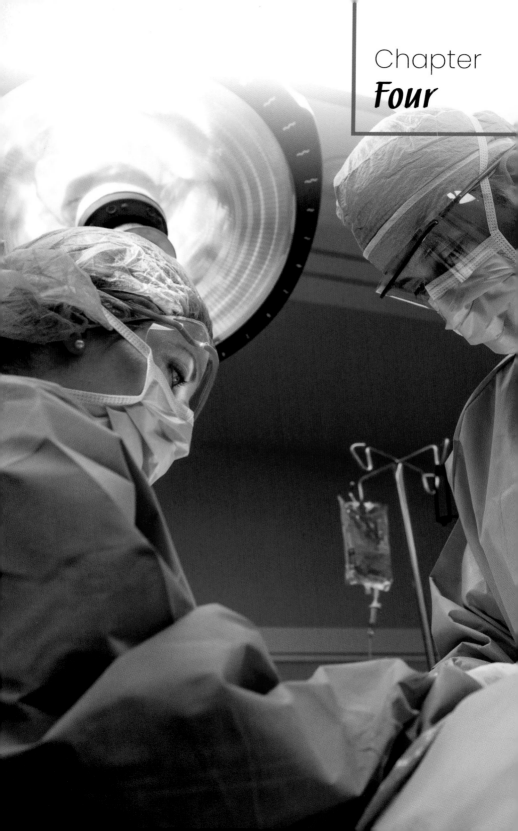

Chapter
Four

Getting Treatment

Once a person has been diagnosed with cancer, a doctor will talk to him or her about a treatment plan. There are many types of cancer treatments. The type of treatment a person receives depends on the type of cancer, where it is located, and how advanced it is. Some people will have only one type of treatment. For most people, however, a combination of treatments will be most effective.

Surgery

If a patient has a solid cancer tumor, doctors may perform surgery to remove it from the body. There are many types of surgery, and each differs based on the cancer's location and how much tissue needs to be removed. If the cancer is limited to one area, a surgeon may be able to remove the entire tumor in a single surgery. Other times, surgeons can remove

Surgery is one common treatment for cancers.

some, but not all, of a cancerous tumor because removing the entire tumor may damage nearby healthy tissue. A surgeon often cannot determine before the surgery whether it will be possible to remove some or all of the tumor. Surgery can also be used to remove tumors that are causing a patient pain or pressure.

Before surgery, a doctor or nurse will talk to a patient about how to prepare for the surgery. A patient may need to get blood tests or X-rays. He or she might not be able to eat or drink for a certain amount of time before the surgery. An empty stomach makes anesthesia—the medications that make a person unconscious during surgery—safer. Food in the stomach can cause complications.

During surgery, the doctor will remove the cancer and will usually also remove some healthy tissues surrounding it. Removing surrounding tissue helps the surgeon make sure that he or she has removed all of the cancer. Sometimes, the surgeon may also remove lymph nodes or other tissue near the cancer. The tissue will be examined under a microscope to see whether there are any cancer cells in it. This information will help doctors recommend the best treatment for a patient after surgery.

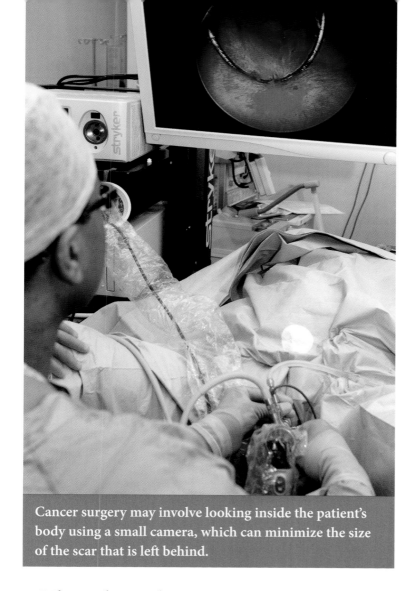

Cancer surgery may involve looking inside the patient's body using a small camera, which can minimize the size of the scar that is left behind.

When Rebecca Blomgren was a teenager, she noticed a bump in her mouth. When she mentioned it to her dentist, he told her it was nothing to worry about. Several years later, when Blomgren was 23 years old, a new dentist diagnosed the lump as oral cancer. The first step in Blomgren's treatment was

Bone Marrow Transplant

To treat some types of blood cancer, a bone marrow transplant is needed. Some cancers, such as leukemia, lymphoma, and multiple myeloma, affect the bone marrow and the body's ability to produce normal blood cells. A bone marrow transplant replaces the patient's bone marrow that has been damaged or destroyed by disease or chemotherapy. In this procedure, doctors transplant healthy blood stem cells into the patient. The stem cells travel to the bone marrow and begin to produce new, healthy blood cells. The transplanted stem cells may be the patient's own stem cells, in what is known as an autologous transplant. They may also be stem cells from a donor, in what is called an allogeneic transplant.

surgery to remove the cancer from her mouth. "In July 2018, I had surgery. The cancer ended up being more advanced than the doctors had originally thought. It had cut into bones, so they had to remove some of my jawbone and four teeth," she says.[1]

Radiation Therapy

Some cancer treatments include radiation therapy. This cancer treatment uses high doses of radiation to kill cancer cells and shrink tumors. The radiation damages the DNA of cancer cells. Eventually, the cancer cells stop dividing or die. When the cancer cells die, the patient's body breaks them down and removes them.

Radiation therapy does not kill cancer cells immediately in a single treatment. Instead, patients receive radiation therapy multiple times over a series of days or weeks. Over time, the radiation treatments damage the cancer cells' DNA enough that they die. The cell death can occur for weeks or months after radiation treatment stops.

During Blomgren's surgery to remove her oral cancer, doctors discovered that the cancer had spread to her nerves. They recommended radiation therapy to destroy any remaining cancer cells that the surgery had not removed. She says,

> *They discovered that parts of the cancer had reached my nerves, which was a concern, because . . . another cancer cell could be further down the line. Having radiation was determined to be the best option for me, and I opted to have proton therapy, a newer type of radiation that is targeted to the cancer cells and does not affect other areas. I wouldn't have to worry about my entire face being subjected to radiation.[2]*

Chemotherapy

Chemotherapy uses drugs to stop or slow the growth of cancer cells. Chemotherapy can be used to eliminate cancer, slow its progression, or reduce the

In radiation therapy, high-tech equipment is used to deliver precisely targeted doses of radiation.

risk of reoccurrence. Sometimes chemotherapy can be used to shrink tumors that are causing pain.

Chemotherapy treatment is used for many cancers. For some people, chemotherapy is the only treatment they need. For others, chemotherapy treatment occurs along with other treatments, such as surgery or radiation therapy. Chemotherapy can make a tumor smaller before surgery. It may also be used after surgery or radiation therapy to destroy any cancer cells remaining in the body.

What Is a Clinical Trial?

A clinical trial is a research study that compares known treatments for a specific type of cancer with a new treatment. That new treatment may be a new medication, a combination of medications, a new therapy, or a new way of using established therapies. Some clinical trials for cancer involve new chemotherapy medications. Others focus on new approaches to surgery and radiation therapy. Some of the most cutting-edge cancer treatments, such as immunotherapy and gene therapy, are undergoing clinical trials. Clinical trials exist for every type of cancer. Some trials focus on treating disease, while others study ways to prevent cancer, stop cancer from returning, reduce side effects, or improve early diagnosis. To participate in a clinical trial, patients may have to meet certain criteria set by the scientists leading the trial.

Side Effects of Treatment

Cancer treatments such as radiation therapy and chemotherapy often have side effects. Some are short-term side effects. They start during treatment and improve when treatment ends. Chemotherapy and radiation kill cancer cells. At the same time, they also kill and damage healthy cells. Often the cells that line the mouth and gastrointestinal tract become damaged. This can lead to sores in the mouth and throat, nausea, vomiting, and diarrhea. Other side effects include dry mouth, loss of appetite and taste, skin rashes, swelling, fatigue, and changes in sleep patterns.

Hair loss is a common side effect of cancer treatment because hair follicles are very sensitive to chemotherapy and radiation. Both of these treatments can cause a person's hair to fall out.

"I often walked around with my [intravenous chemotherapy stand] as the chemotherapy flooded my veins; I felt alone. It's like how they tell you that 'sometimes, you can be the most alone in a crowded room.'"[3]

—Alex, *a patient diagnosed with Ewing sarcoma*

In many cases, hair loss is temporary. People will usually notice their hair beginning to regrow a few months after finishing treatment. In some cases, hair loss may be permanent. When 24-year-old Mia Brister's hair began to fall out during treatment for Hodgkin's lymphoma, she was devastated. "As treatment progressed, my hair began to fall out. I cried for days trying to figure out how I would look without my hair, how people would see me without it, and I wondered, would my melon head really look good bald? It crushed me the day I decided to cut and shave it all off. People would reassure me that it's just hair, and that it would grow back, but part of my identity was gone," she says.[4]

When Ruth Wawszczyk was 14 years old, she was diagnosed with anaplastic large cell lymphoma. After her diagnosis, she began treatment with intensive chemotherapy. Her cancer responded to treatment, but she began to experience side effects from the chemotherapy. "At one time my mouth and digestive tract were so ulcerated that I had to have my food pureed like a baby's. I suffered from boils which flared up rapidly and needed treating with intravenous antibiotics. I also got terrible pains in various parts of my body and couldn't even turn over in bed without help," she says.

She explains,

> *The large amounts of hydration used to flush the chemotherapy drugs through my body caused my heart to race audibly. My blood pressure rose during each week of intensive treatment so that I used to worry that I would not be allowed home on . . . Saturday night. I became painfully constipated. I also experienced a terrible headache after one of the intrathecal injections of methotrexate.[5]*

Other side effects can emerge months or years after treatment. Some chemotherapy drugs or radiation treatment to the chest may make a person more likely to have heart or lung problems in the future. Some treatments affect the endocrine system and can cause hormone problems or infertility. Chemotherapy and radiation treatments can also cause long-term damage to the bones, joints, and soft tissues, as well as the brain and nervous system. Other long-term side effects from cancer treatment include problems with learning, memory,

"Chemotherapy is hard. I was tired and weak and pushed beyond my physical limits."[6]

—A cancer patient diagnosed with non-Hodgkin's lymphoma

and attention. Cancer treatment may also make a person more likely to develop secondary cancers in the future.

Every person's reaction to cancer treatment is different. Two people receiving the same treatments may experience different side effects. No one can predict which side effects will affect a person or how intense they will be. Patients should talk to their doctor or nurse about any side effects they are experiencing so that their medical team can take steps to reduce those effects.

Finding Support

Everyone deals with cancer in their own way. A person may think that he or she can handle everything alone, but sometimes living with cancer can be tough physically and emotionally. A person may end up needing help with everyday tasks. He or she may simply feel lonely or afraid and need to talk to someone. That's why building a support network is important when handling cancer.

Building a Support Network

Support for cancer patients can come from many places. It may come from family, friends, a therapist, or a support group of other cancer patients and survivors. Asking for help can be hard, especially if a person is independent, but it's important to speak up. A patient's family and friends may want to assist but might not know what to do. Often they can help with

Talking to friends is one way to find support when dealing with cancer.

everyday tasks such as cleaning or running errands. A trusted family member or friend might go with the patient to doctor appointments and treatments. People might help by making meals or putting together care packages.

For patients with religious beliefs, their faith and the support of their faith community can be important. Jason, who has chronic myelogenous leukemia, says he has relied on family, friends, and his faith for support since his cancer diagnosis: "My faith in God and my family and friends have been my greatest support. I'm not afraid to talk about it anymore. I talk about it openly. I take it one day at a time and put my life in God's hands."[1]

Camps for Cancer Families

There are camps across the country that run programs for childhood cancer patients and their families. These facilities offer summer camps, weeklong retreats, and weekend programs. They typically charge patients and families very little. Some are even free to attend. Doctors and nurses are on-site to provide medical care to campers if needed. Many camps also have staff who can provide care to children with special needs.

Finding others who understand what patients and their families are going through at camp can be invaluable. Attending a camp makes cancer patients feel less different than they do with their friends at home. Many make lasting friendships with other campers they meet.

People's faith traditions may be key sources of support in their fight with cancer.

When Allison was 16 years old, she was diagnosed with tumors in her kidney and adrenal gland. It wasn't her first fight with cancer; she had already been treated at age three for a brain tumor and recovered. Allison's family and friends pulled together to help her and her parents. Her mother wrote "Alli Rocks" with window markers on her hospital room window. Every visitor signed the windows so Allison could see the names of every person rooting for her. They plastered the walls of her room with pictures of family and friends. Extended family and friends pitched in to provide meals for the family, and Allison's sisters came to her doctor appointments to take notes and speak up for their sister's needs. "I carried the whole burden the first time, so this time I decided to let people help," said Karen, Allison's mother. "It feels like our family is one big unit huddled around Allison, fiercely protecting her. We really are a force to be reckoned with."[2]

Elizabeth was diagnosed with Ewing sarcoma at 15. This type of cancer forms in bone or soft tissue. Many people stepped up to help Elizabeth and her family through her cancer journey. Church friends prepared meals for the family and donated food-delivery gift cards so she did not have to eat hospital food.

"If I've learned anything from this involuntary experience, it's that your true friends and supporters will emerge in full force."[4]

—Mary Best, a patient diagnosed with cancer

As she looks back on her experience, Elizabeth remembers one friend in particular who knew how to give her both comfort and the space to discuss her cancer only if she wanted to. "I was diagnosed around Christmas time. . . . My mom had texted my friend's mom about my diagnosis, and my friend texted me and just said 'I'm thinking about you—we don't have to talk about it unless you want to, we can just have fun tonight.' That day, that text was exactly what I needed," she says.[3]

Support Groups

Sometimes it helps to talk with other people who are also coping with cancer. In a support group, people living with cancer can talk with others, sharing their feelings and experiences with people who are going through the same health challenges. Support group participants share what worked for them, celebrate important milestones in their treatment, and talk about issues they have experienced related to their cancer. "Support groups can be effective in many ways," says clinical social worker Claire J. Casselman. "Meeting and talking with other people whose lives are affected by cancer can create a sense of community or commonness that helps relieve the stress of isolation

Support for Caregivers

Being a caregiver for a person with cancer can be very challenging. Many caregivers put their own needs, feelings, and lives aside so they can focus their energy on helping the person with cancer. Over time, this stress can affect the caregiver's physical and psychological health. That's why it is important for caregivers of cancer patients to put aside some time to take care of themselves. Some strategies include finding time to relax each day, not neglecting their own personal lives, keeping a routine, and asking others for help from time to time. Some caregivers may find it helpful to join a support group specifically formed for caregivers of cancer patients.

that many people experience."[5] When participants listen to the stories of other group members and talk about themselves, they realize that many of their feelings and reactions are common for people in their situation. They exchange practical advice for day-to-day life and might open their minds to new perspectives on living with cancer.

Gailon is an ambassador for Teen Cancer America (TCA). After she was diagnosed with small round blue cell undifferentiated sarcoma, she found help in a support group:

Hearing stories from other people affected by cancer has been immensely helpful for me. After my diagnosis, I felt like I had gone to a place none of my friends had been to before and no matter how hard I tried to describe it and how willing they were to try to understand, it was still an isolating experience. Meeting other young adult cancer patients and survivors gave me the validation that I am not the only person who has felt the way that I did. There are few things that have brought me as much comfort as hearing someone say, "that happened to you too!?"[6]

Many people feel nervous about joining a support group. "Some people have a fear about opening up and telling others their story or hearing others' experiences," says Joan Hermann, a director of social work in Philadelphia, Pennsylvania. "They may think a support group may make them even more depressed."[7] However, in Hermann's experience, participating in a support group helps cancer patients feel less alone. In addition, offering support to others can help patients feel better about themselves. Jason is one patient who found these benefits: "I go to the support group once a month and that's been a great help. Each time we go there's someone new who has just been diagnosed. We share our experiences and what we're going through. I want to get involved with

Support groups allow patients to share their experiences and offer help to one another.

the Leukemia Lymphoma Society so I can help others who have cancer."[8]

Support groups come in several forms. Some are for cancer patients only, while others include patients and their spouse or caregiver. Other support groups give caregivers a forum to discuss their experiences. Group meetings may be held in person or online. Often a patient's doctor or care team can recommend support groups and can help a patient find a group that is reputable and led by a trained facilitator.

"The first time I opened up was when I attended Camp Ronald McDonald. . . . There were others there going through the same thing I was and it felt like a breath of fresh air, to instantly connect with a stranger through sharing similar experiences."[9]

—Alyssa, a cancer survivor

Counseling and Therapy

Living with cancer can make people feel anxious, worried, and overwhelmed. They may struggle with feelings of isolation and depression. Some patients may find it helpful to talk to a social worker, therapist, or counselor about what they are experiencing. There are counselors and therapists who are specially trained to work with people who have cancer.

Therapy provides a safe space for people living with cancer to talk about anything that is troubling them. They can learn healthy ways to process their feelings as well as ways to cope with a cancer diagnosis and feel more in control of their life. They may learn strategies to help them deal with depression and anxiety or manage cancer's symptoms and side effects. They can talk about fears of how cancer might change their lives or discuss any relationship issues they are having with family and friends.

Patients may choose different types of therapy depending on their needs and preferences. Some therapy is individual. Patients meet one-on-one with a trained counselor to talk about their feelings,

Online Support Groups

Some people with cancer join online support groups. These groups have online meetings using chat rooms, email lists, webinars, social media, or moderated discussion groups. Because of their online format, participants can take part whenever their schedule allows. For people who live in rural areas or who cannot easily travel to in-person meetings, online support groups can be a good option. Because not all groups are monitored, patients should check any information or advice they receive from group members with their doctors.

concerns, and problems. The counselor listens, asks questions, and provides feedback. In family therapy, the patient and family members meet together with a counselor. The counselor listens to each person and tries to help the family resolve any conflicts or issues they have. Together, family members learn ways to support each other. In group therapy, several people with cancer may meet together with a counselor. The counselor will lead the discussion and provide support to the group. Group members learn how to express their feelings and learn coping strategies from the counselor and each other.

How Cancer Affects Daily Life

Cancer affects a person in many ways. Many people have good days and bad days, depending on where they are in treatment and which side effects they experience. Knowing what to expect can help a person manage daily life with cancer.

Physical Effects

When going through cancer treatment, a person might find that he or she does not feel well during treatment and for a few hours or days afterward. Many people find that they feel tired during and after chemotherapy or radiation treatment. They may not have the energy to follow their usual routine and take part in activities that they usually enjoy. Instead, they

Hair loss, a result of chemotherapy, is one visible sign that a person has been treated for cancer.

Pet Therapy

Pet therapy is growing in popularity for people with cancer. Patients spend time with emotional support animals, which are often dogs. The animals' presence provides many physical and emotional benefits for patients. Patients with chronic pain have shown a decreased need for pain medication. Other benefits of pet therapy are lowered stress levels, improved mood, decreased anxiety, reduced loneliness and feelings of isolation, and a sense of emotional connection. Researchers believe that therapy dogs may cause a decrease in levels of cortisol, the stress hormone, in a patient's blood. Pet therapy may also increase another type of hormone in the body called endorphins, which act as the body's natural pain relievers.

may need to slow down their pace of life and take some extra time to rest and restore their body. To do this, they may need to take some time off of work or school and get family and friends to help with chores around the house.

Treatment may also disrupt a person's daily eating habits. The person may experience nausea, vomiting, or loss of appetite after chemotherapy. If this happens, it might be easier to eat small, bland meals or high-calorie nutritional drinks instead of larger meals. After a few days, a person may begin to feel better and be able to get back to his or her usual daily activities.

Changing Appearance

Cancer and its treatment can cause a person's appearance to change. Chemotherapy and radiation can cause a person to lose hair, gain or lose weight, or have dry, itchy skin. Surgeries can leave scars. Breast cancer patients may have one or both breasts removed. Some bone cancer patients may have life-saving limb amputations.

Patients may struggle with these changes and their effects on body image and self-esteem. Even if changes are not visible to others, they can still affect how patients see themselves and how they interact with others. They might feel self-conscious or embarrassed. They may feel as if everyone is staring at them. These feelings may cause a person to not

Journaling

Some cancer patients find that journaling or creative writing is a way for them to express their feelings about cancer. Some people find writing helps them relieve stress. Others want to record their thoughts and feelings during their cancer journey. Writing can also help a person clarify thoughts or let go of anger and resentment. Those who focus on writing about positive thoughts find that journaling can help them see the silver linings in their experience. While not everyone chooses to journal their cancer experience, it can be helpful for those who do.

want to go out in public or not want to date or meet new people. They might avoid undressing in front of others, or they might try to hide scars. When feeling self-conscious about a changing appearance, a person might decide to wear a wig, hat, or scarf to cover hair loss. Some decide to try new makeup, hairstyles, or clothing to help them feel better about their changing appearance.

Emotional Effects

Just as cancer affects a person physically, it can also cause a roller coaster of emotions. Existing emotions may feel more intense than before. Moods may change day by day, hour by hour, or even minute by minute. Cancer can also trigger a variety of emotions that a person is not used to dealing with, such as anxiety, despair, and depression. A person may feel overwhelmed and be in denial about the cancer. He or she may feel angry, afraid, worried, stressed, lonely, and sad. These emotions

"I would tell another kid going through cancer that it will get easier. And there are ways to enjoy stuff still. I like doing art when I'm here for chemo. It's really fun."[1]

—*Ella, a patient diagnosed with ALL*

Intense anger or sadness are natural for a person who has been diagnosed with cancer.

Music Therapy

In good times, music can have a big effect on a person. It can make a person happier and lower stress levels. Cancer patients can also use music to help them handle day-to-day life with cancer. The emotions of living with cancer can be intense. Several studies have shown that music can help reduce anxiety, improve mood, improve quality of life, help manage pain, and even reduce shortness of breath. Music can also have some physical benefits for patients, including decreasing heart and respiratory rates and lowering blood pressure. Recognizing the power of music, there are now dozens of cancer centers that incorporate music therapy into their treatments.

can last throughout treatment, and they can even linger long after the person has completed treatment. While it may feel overwhelming at times, all of these swirling emotions are completely normal when living with cancer. "It helped a lot that my family was adamant about allowing me to feel whatever I felt," says Rebecca Blomgren. "Sometimes I would get angry at the situation, and I would misdirect the anger at my family. When I later apologized, my parents always told me I had nothing to apologize for. They let me know that if I needed to cry or yell, or just sit on the couch all day and not say a word, that was fine, and they were not going to hold it against me."[2]

While being treated for ALL at age 17, Patrick Eck struggled with depression. He says,

On the outside, I maintained a brave face, and my family and friends commented on how strong I was. However, on the inside, I was filled with the fear of death and the possibility that even if I lived, my life would never be the same. I was jealous as I watched my friends start their senior year, get ready for college, and go on dates. Would I ever have a girlfriend? I wondered. After all, who would want someone whose body—and soul— were ravaged by cancer?[3]

Managing Cancer Day by Day

"Whether you are in the middle of treatment, completing treatment, or newly diagnosed, trust that you will get to a place where you can say, 'I'm happy, and I am alive.'"[4]

—*A young woman diagnosed with cancer*

Being diagnosed with cancer is a life-changing event. Learning how to adjust to a new normal can be challenging. But just because people have cancer does not mean they have to stop living life or doing many of the activities they enjoy. In fact, most doctors

Riding for Health

In 2015 high school sophomore Matthew Simon was diagnosed with leukemia. Simon was a crew rower who worked out daily. During his first three-week stay in the hospital for treatment, he walked laps around the floor when he felt strong enough. But Simon longed for some other way to move his body. The hospital staff found a virtual reality bike and moved it into his room. Simon rode the bike daily. After his initial round of treatment, Simon transferred to another hospital where he spent several days at a time doing additional rounds of inpatient treatment. He rode an exercise bike there too. Simon says that keeping active and riding the bike helped him fight the fatigue brought on by his chemotherapy and helped to lift his mood. To him, riding the bike was one way he could help himself stay healthy during treatment.

recommend that cancer patients keep to their normal daily routines if they feel well enough, including going to work or school, spending time with family and friends, participating in activities, and traveling. "My cancer made me take a closer look at how I spend my days. I vowed to use my time in ways that were good for me or brought me pleasure," says Lindsay, a cancer patient.[5]

Eating healthy is important for all people, but it is especially crucial for those who are living with cancer. The body needs to get enough calories and nutrients to be strong during treatment. However, cancer and the side effects from treatment can make it difficult to get the nutrients a person needs before, during, and after treatment. A person might not feel like eating or he or she may experience nausea or vomiting. The foods a person used to like may not taste the same anymore. The mouth and gastrointestinal tract may be irritated, making it painful to eat certain foods. That's why it is important to fill the body with healthful foods, especially those that need little preparation. Nuts, applesauce, yogurt, and whole grains are easy and healthful options. High-protein foods such as lean meat, chicken, fish, eggs, beans, nuts, and dairy products provide important nutrients. Colorful vegetables and fruits are good choices too.

Cancer and School

Each year, more than 15,000 people under the age of 20 are diagnosed with cancer in the United States, according to the Centers for Disease Control and Prevention (CDC).[1] Most of those kids will go to school for at least part of the time while they are in cancer treatment and after their treatment. For these patients, living with cancer and going to school can present some unique challenges.

Staying Connected

For most students, school is a central part of daily life. School is where they learn, have fun, and make friends. Continuing to be connected with school activities is beneficial during cancer treatment. It helps children and teens continue to learn and grow, keeps them connected with their life before cancer,

Cancer in kids and teens can have a significant effect on their education.

and can help them feel less overwhelmed when they eventually return to school.

How a student deals with school activities depends on his or her type of cancer and treatment plan. There are several options families can discuss with doctors, hospital education coordinators, and school teachers. If the student is not going to return to school for a long time, the school district might have a teacher come to the home. When a patient named Allison was 13 years old, she was diagnosed with osteogenic sarcoma, a type of bone cancer. "Being removed from school during the 8th grade was difficult, but with the support of my family and friends, I was home-tutored and was able to graduate with my class. I cannot express how much that means to me," she says.[2]

> "I find the hardest part of being pulled out of college to battle cancer is the feeling of being left behind."[3]
>
> —Jordan, a patient diagnosed with Hodgkin's lymphoma

If a student is going to be in the hospital for a long period, teachers from school or hospital staff might provide instruction at the hospital. This option often works well for students who do not feel well enough

Neuropsychology Testing

Cancer and its treatments can cause learning problems. Most students who have been treated for cancer will benefit from neuropsychology testing. This testing can be done by a school psychologist or counselor, or it can be done at the patient's cancer treatment center. It helps identify the child's individual learning needs. Neuropsychology testing usually measures academic skills, such as reading, writing, and math, along with more general skills, such as memory, comprehension, attention, concentration, and fine motor control. If testing shows that a student needs extra help, families and schools can work together to develop a plan to address his or her learning needs.

or have the stamina for long school days. They can still feel connected to their old life even with just an hour of schooling per day.

Tutors can help kids with serious medical challenges keep up with schoolwork.

Returning to School During Treatment

At some point during their cancer treatment, some students return to traditional school for at least part of the time. This typically depends on their treatment schedule, how they feel, and their risk of infection. Doctors can help families determine when it is safe for a student being treated for cancer to return to school. Many will not be able return to school full-time during treatment but may be able

Chemo Brain

Many patients complain about mental cloudiness that they notice during and after cancer treatment. This cloudiness is commonly called chemo brain. Most people describe it as not being able to remember things and having trouble finishing tasks, concentrating, or learning new skills. Chemo brain is commonly linked to chemotherapy, but other cancer treatments, such as radiation and surgery, can be linked to it as well. For most people, the mental changes of chemo brain generally occur during and just after treatment. For some, it continues after treatment ends. Chemo brain can make it harder for a student to focus and learn new things in school. Students can work to manage chemo brain with strategies such as using a daily planner or reminder notes, getting plenty of rest, exercising the brain, getting regular physical exercise, setting and following routines, and keeping track of any memory problems that occur.

to spend some time in the classroom when they are feeling well.

Returning to school during cancer treatment can be scary for some kids. Doctors and other members of the care team can help make the transition a little bit easier. Before students return to school, a member of their care team can go to the school, talk to teachers and classmates about cancer, and answer any questions they may have. They can also arrange meetings with school administrators and teachers to make sure the student has the support and accommodations he or she needs to learn. The cancer care team can also talk to teachers and nurses about how to manage side effects such as fatigue, nausea, or pain during the school day.

"I had to attend physical therapy and strength building classes during the summer before returning to school in 10th grade. I had to regain muscle that I lost during treatment so I could walk a full day in school."[4]

—Alyssa, a cancer survivor

When she was in eighth grade, Lily was diagnosed with ALL. "During her [first] 11 months of treatment, Lily missed a lot of school due to her treatment schedules and low immunity," says her mother,

Michelle. "The school was so generous and worked with us to make sure Lily was ready to start grade nine in the fall. They also made sure to schedule subjects in the first semester that [were] easier for her to do independently. Now that she's back in school as full time as possible, Lily has realized how much she missed the interaction with other students and teachers."[5]

Some students may feel apprehensive about returning to school during or after cancer treatment. They might be worried about how their friends and classmates will react to their changing appearance.

Learning Plans

When a student has learning problems from cancer treatment, parents and teachers may work together to develop a plan to meet his or her individual learning needs. If the student meets the legal requirements to qualify as a special education student, the plan is known as an Individual Education Plan (IEP). If the student does not qualify for an IEP, a 504 Plan, named for the section of the law that it comes from, may be used. Both plan types describe a student's learning problems and set specific education goals. They include referrals to other services or therapies, such as speech therapy. They may include learning accommodations for the student. For example, a student may need more time to complete assignments or need to take tests in a quiet room. Both IEPs and 504 Plans will be reviewed regularly. The plans can be updated if the child's needs change.

They might be stressed about catching up on the schoolwork that they missed. They might also find it difficult to adjust to a new routine or changes in their abilities. Often, parents and the cancer care team can discuss these fears with the student before he or she returns. They can help develop strategies to deal with different situations at school. Knowing how to handle a situation and whom to talk to about it can help a kid feel more in control of his or her situation.

When 16-year-old Jenn returned to school after being treated for acute myeloid leukemia, she chose not to wear anything on her bald head. "People just had to get used to seeing me look different. I was the same old Jenn, I just had a new look," she says. "When I went back to school it was very overwhelming at first. But seeing my friends and talking to them made it a lot easier." Even so, Jenn says she struggled to get back into schoolwork. "My teachers were very understanding and willing to work with me so that was good and a big help," says Jenn.[6]

A cancer diagnosis can have a big impact on regular school routines. Yet with some help and planning, many students can continue learning during treatment and return to school full-time once they have completed treatment.

Living as a Survivor

When patients reach the end of cancer treatment and their cancer is in remission, they are ready to start the next part of their lives. In 2016, there were approximately 15.5 million cancer survivors in the United States according to the National Cancer Institute (NCI).[1] By 2026, there are expected to be 20.3 million survivors.[2] For cancer survivors, some days are full of hope and excitement for future plans. Other times, survivors struggle with fear and worry, which may intensify around the time of routine checkups. For each person, living as a survivor is a different experience.

Making the Transition to Survivor

While virtually all cancer patients are happy when their treatment is finally over, they may feel

Surviving cancer may prompt both celebration and anxiety.

Stages of Survivorship

Fitzhugh Mullan, a doctor who was diagnosed with cancer himself, described cancer survivorship as occurring in three stages. The first, acute survivorship, begins at diagnosis and lasts until the end of the patient's initial treatment plan. In this phase, the focus of the patient and doctors is treating the cancer. Next, the patient moves into extended survivorship, the period following the end of initial treatment. In this phase, the patient and his or her care team are watchful for signs of the cancer returning. They focus on the lingering effects of cancer and the treatment. The final stage is permanent survivorship. It occurs when the chances of the cancer returning are extremely low. In this final phase, the patient may be able to return to a more ordinary life, but he or she may still be dealing with lingering psychological and physical effects from the experience.

unprepared for some of the challenges as they transition to post-treatment care. Cancer survivor Maya Harsaniova explains, "As a cancer survivor, I have found that there is no manual or guide that offers a road map on what I am supposed to feel, or how I should act, once I heard these words from my oncologist, 'You are cancer free.'"[3]

Even though their cancer is gone, many survivors still have weeks, months, and even years of follow-up care. This care can be frustrating if new problems, whether related or unrelated to the cancer, appear. Doctors will monitor patients to make sure their cancer stays in remission and will examine and treat them for any cancer-related or treatment-related side effects. Some survivors deal with long-term side effects from the cancer or treatment for years.

Cancer survivors are used to seeing their doctors and cancer care team frequently. When treatment is finished, they may visit less frequently. Not seeing the people who have helped them through a difficult period in their lives might make survivors anxious or sad.

Some cancer survivors find that getting back into their pre-cancer role in their family is not as simple as they thought it would be. Things they did before cancer might have been taken over by others. Teen survivors may want to reassert their independence,

Worries about lingering side effects and cancer returning can lead to intense stress.

which may set up conflict with worried parents who are still feeling protective over their child.

Some survivors find that many of the emotions they dealt with during treatment become more intense. They feel overwhelmed, sad, angry, or afraid. Some of these feelings could be lingering side effects from treatment. They could also be a sign that a person's body and mind need some rest and relaxation. These feelings are normal. The American Cancer Society's website notes, "Facing these feelings and learning how to deal with them is important. Don't expect everything to go back to the way it

Survivors in College

Cancer survivors going off to college face unique challenges. For many, it is the first time since their cancer diagnosis when they will be on their own, away from parents and family. These young adults will have to take charge of their own health and be proactive about setting up the resources and support they may need while away from home. Before arriving on campus, survivors should plan ahead for any cancer-related concerns or issues they may have at college. They may still suffer from side effects, or new side effects may emerge while they are away. If they will need accommodations in class, they should talk to the college before class begins to get everything ready. They should also inform advisors or other college officials of their medical history. That way the school may be better able to help the student in the event of a medical emergency.

was before you were diagnosed. Give yourself, your family, and those around you time. . . . You'll get through this. Just like it took time to adjust to cancer, you can adjust to life after cancer."[4]

Will Cancer Come Back?

Some cancers can come back after treatment. The chances of cancer recurring depend on many variables, such as the type of cancer, where it was located, and what stage it was. Cancer can recur in the same place, or it might return in another place in the body. While it is difficult to predict whether a cancer will return, it is more likely to come back if it was fast growing or widespread.

For cancer survivors and their families, worry that their cancer may return is common and normal. Many cancer survivors find they pay a lot of attention to any aches or pains in their body. They worry their cancer is back and wonder how to know for

"I was so afraid of a relapse, I avoided going to my oncologist for checkups. I wanted to run away from cancer and all that fear and pain. But at the same time, I felt fearless. I had just beaten cancer."[5]

—*Hernan Barangan, a survivor of acute myeloid leukemia*

certain if it does return. Although this fear can be intense, many survivors find that as time passes and they remain healthy, the fear of their cancer coming back decreases. They find themselves thinking about cancer less. However, certain events may cause the fear to reemerge, such as follow-up medical tests, an anniversary of their diagnosis date, or learning that someone they know has cancer.

Financial Hardship

According to survey data published in 2020 in a journal of the American Association for Cancer Research, a majority of US cancer survivors face significant financial hardship, especially those age 64 and younger. According to survey respondents, financial hardships included problems paying medical bills, financial distress, or delaying or skipping medical care entirely due to payment concerns. Participants were also forced to make financial sacrifices, including changes in spending habits and the use of savings to pay for medical care and day-to-day expenses.

Late Effects of Cancer

Cancer treatments such as chemotherapy and radiation can cause health problems for survivors later on. The medications and treatments used to kill cancer cells sometimes also damage healthy cells and tissue. Sometimes, delayed effects do not emerge until years after treatment. For example, radiation therapy to treat head and neck cancer can lead to dental problems and bone disease years after treatment.

Cancer survivors should understand which treatments they received could put them at risk for long-term health problems. Survivors should know how to recognize those problems and what they should do if the issues emerge. They should also learn what they can do to keep themselves healthy.

Dr. Robert Goldsby is a pediatric cancer specialist and the director of his hospital's cancer survivor program. On understanding prior therapies as a survivor, he says:

> *I think it's paramount for survivors to advocate for themselves and advocate for other survivors, and I think one of the ways to do that is to learn and know what your therapies were and what your risks are. . . . Some survivors are done with their cancer, and they don't want to have anything to do with cancer and they feel like, that part of my life is gone and I'm going to live life. I applaud the enthusiasm for life in survivors, but I also do think it is important for all survivors to have some documented summary of their therapy.*[6]

Taking Care of Body and Mind

Battling cancer can be rough on the body and mind. For cancer survivors, several simple lifestyle choices can help improve their health and quality of life after cancer. Exercise can improve a survivor's sense of well-being and accelerate recovery after cancer treatment. Exercise has physical benefits, such as increased strength and endurance. It can also improve a person's mood, decrease anxiety, and reduce symptoms of depression. Regular exercise can also fight fatigue and improve sleep habits.

"Cancer changed me. It took a lot from me, but I did gain a little bit. I'm one of the 'lucky' ones, and I recognize this daily. My life is relatively back to normal. I don't have any lingering side effects, and so far, so good."[7]

—*Samantha, a survivor of osteosarcoma*

Exercise can start small and gradually increase in intensity over time as the person is able. The American Cancer Society recommends that adult cancer survivors exercise for at least 150 minutes each week, including strength training two days a week. In addition, some scientific

Staying active is important for anyone, but it can have particular benefits for people who have survived cancer.

studies suggest that exercise may even reduce the risk of cancer recurring. Other lifestyle choices, such as eating a balanced diet, maintaining a healthy weight, getting enough sleep, reducing stress, and staying away from tobacco and alcohol, can also help survivors improve their quality of life after cancer.

Eating Right

Eating right can help cancer survivors feel their best. The American Cancer Society recommends that cancer survivors eat a balanced diet, which includes a lot of fruits, vegetables, and whole grains. They recommend that survivors eat two to three cups of fruits and vegetables daily. They should also eat low-fat proteins, whole grains, and healthy fats. Although there is no evidence that a particular diet can reduce the risk of cancer returning, eating right can help people feel their best and can reduce the risk of obesity, heart disease, and other conditions.

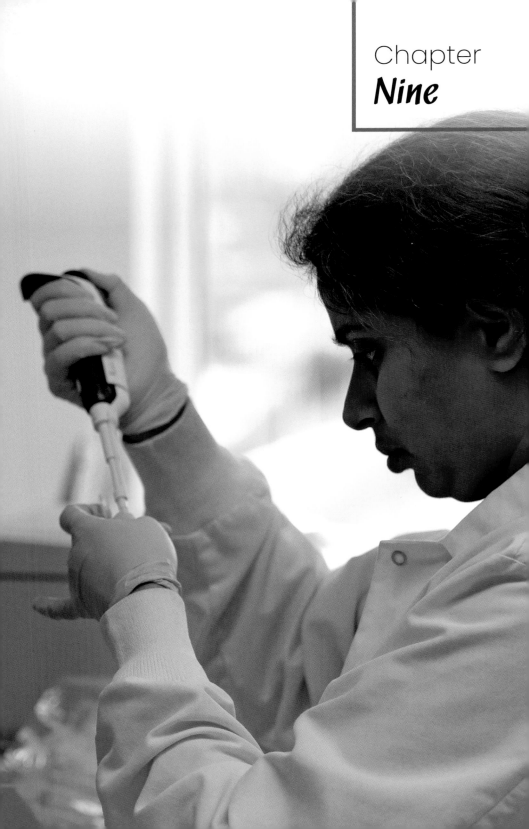

Treatment Evolves

Across the world, scientists are studying cancer to better understand how it starts, how it progresses, and how to treat it. Their knowledge of cancer is constantly growing through cutting-edge research. They are developing new and more effective ways to prevent, detect, diagnose, and treat various types of cancers.

Immunotherapy

The body's immune system is a powerful fighter against infection and disease. Finding ways to use the immune system to better recognize and attack cancer cells has been a major focus in cancer research in recent years. A type of cancer treatment called immunotherapy helps the body's immune system fight cancer. It is a type of biological therapy, which means that it uses substances from living organisms

Researchers are exploring new ways to combat the many different forms of cancer.

to fight cancer. It is a relatively recent treatment, but it has already revolutionized cancer therapy by improving survival rates and expanding treatment options.

The immune system works by detecting and destroying abnormal cells in the body. This response likely prevents the growth of many cancers. Sometimes, the immune system does not recognize cancer cells as something to attack, since the cells came from the patient's own body. In other cases, cancer cells have ways to actively avoid the immune system. These factors can allow cancer cells to divide and spread in the body. Immunotherapy helps the immune system recognize a person's cancer as an enemy and attack it.

The Food and Drug Administration (FDA) has approved several immunotherapy treatments to treat a number of different cancer types. One class of immunotherapy drugs is known as immune checkpoint inhibitors. They help the body's immune

Cancer Vaccines

Scientists are studying cancer vaccines as a way to help the body's immune system fight cancer. Some vaccines are made from cancer cells removed from a patient during surgery. The killed cancer cells are processed in a lab to make them more recognizable to the body's immune system. Then they are reinjected into the patient. This prepares the patient's immune system to launch an attack on the injected cancer cells and other similar cancer cells in the body. Other vaccines are made by removing some of a patient's white blood cells. In a lab, scientists expose the cells to a protein from the cancer. When reinjected into the patient, the white cells are primed to attack the cancer cells.

system properly recognize and respond to cancer cells. "With the use of immune checkpoint inhibitors, we've been able to see that the immune system can treat many different types of cancer, regardless of where they originate," says Dr. Padmanee Sharma, an immunologist and oncologist at the University of Texas. "However, not all patients respond to this therapeutic strategy, and not every tumor type responds in the way that we expect. We must work diligently to improve the number of patients that can benefit from immunotherapeutic approaches."[2]

Another area of research involves the use of immunotherapy in combination with other treatments. "Immune checkpoint inhibitors can be

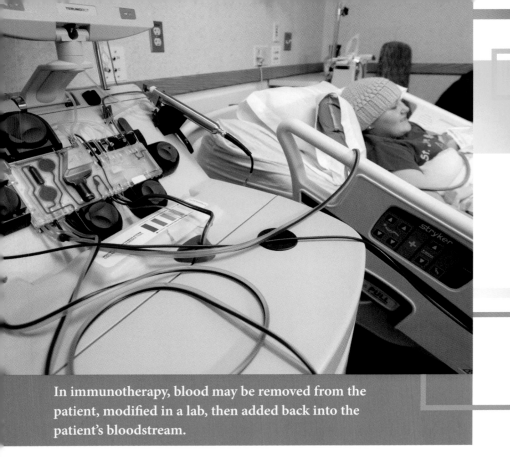

In immunotherapy, blood may be removed from the patient, modified in a lab, then added back into the patient's bloodstream.

combined with a host of other therapeutic strategies," Sharma says. Treatments that target cancer cells directly, such as chemotherapy or radiation therapy, could potentially be used as a first step. "An immune checkpoint inhibitor can then enhance the T-cell killing of the remaining cancerous cells," she says.[3]

CAR T-Cell Therapy

Another promising immunotherapy approach is adoptive cell transfer (ACT). This therapy collects and uses a patient's own immune cells to treat the cancer. One particular type of ACT therapy, called chimeric antigen receptor (CAR) T-cell therapy, has shown promise in patients with advanced blood cancers. CAR T-cell therapy is a treatment in which the immune system's T cells are altered in a lab so they will attack cancer cells. To do so, the T cells are first removed from a patient's blood. Then scientists add a gene to the T cells. This gene codes for a special receptor that binds to a protein on the patient's cancer cells. Scientists grow large numbers of the altered CAR T cells in the lab. Then they transfer those cells to the patient.

In 2017, the FDA approved two CAR T-cell therapies for the treatment of children with acute lymphoblastic leukemia (ALL) and for the treatment of adults with advanced lymphoma. Researchers are still working on ways to use this type of therapy against solid tumors, such as those seen in breast and colorectal cancers. However, in recent years, progress using CAR T cells and other ACT therapies has advanced quickly as researchers gain a better understanding of how these therapies work in patients and use that knowledge for further development and testing. "In the next few years, I think we're going to see dramatic progress and push

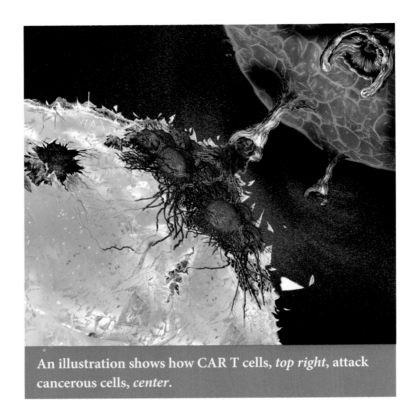

An illustration shows how CAR T cells, *top right*, attack cancerous cells, *center*.

the boundaries of what many people thought was possible with these adoptive cell transfer–based treatments," says Dr. Steven Rosenberg, a surgeon and immunotherapy expert at the NCI's Center for Cancer Research (CCR).[4] Rosenberg's lab was the first to report successful cancer treatment with CAR T cells.

Gene Therapy

Some scientists are focusing on the use of gene therapy to treat or prevent cancer by changing the genetic instructions in a person's cells. In humans, genes hold the body's genetic instructions. These instructions contain the code to build the proteins that enable cells to function, grow, and divide. When a gene is defective, it can lead to errors in this process. When a gene is missing or overactive, critical proteins may not be built, disrupting important body functions. Gene therapy aims to fix these problems by altering a person's genes.

In gene therapy, scientists attempt to replace abnormal or missing genes with healthy ones. With these changes, a person's cells would then be able to build fully functioning proteins. Gene therapy can also change the way genes are regulated, which means how they are turned on or off, so that overactive or underactive genes can function properly.

Researchers are studying a number of ways to use gene therapy in cancer treatment. Most studies are in preliminary stages. Areas that are being investigated include using genetically engineered viruses to directly kill cancer cells and transferring genes into cancer cells or surrounding tissue. These genes either cause the cancer cells to die or prevent the nearby tissue from providing blood to tumors, starving them and preventing them from growing.

Precision Medicine

Precision medicine, which is the personalized tailoring of treatment based on an individual's cancer, is an area of cancer treatment that is expected to expand in the future. Today, doctors are able to use cancer's biomarkers to determine whether a patient has a good chance of responding to a particular treatment plan. However, scientists are working to make precision medicine even more individualized. The hope is that one day cancer treatments will be tailored to the genetic mutations and changes in each person's individual cancer. In the future, genetic testing of cancer may guide doctors in selecting the treatments a patient is most likely to benefit from, eliminating time wasted on treatments that do not work.

Liquid Biopsy Tests

In the future, doctors may be able to diagnose cancer with a simple blood test. Liquid biopsy tests detect and identify cancer biomarkers, or substances that indicate the presence of a particular disease, in a person's blood or spinal fluid. With cancer, biomarkers are commonly cancer tumor cells, tumor DNA, and other tumor materials. Because liquid biopsies detect a tumor's genetic makeup, they can also be used to select the most appropriate treatment.

The limited amount of tumor biomarkers in blood plasma or spinal fluid has made this type of test difficult. However, advances in technologies to detect and read even the smallest amount of tumor biomarkers have improved the accuracy of liquid biopsy tests. Scientists hope that one day this type of test will be widely available to diagnose cancer and eliminate the need for more invasive needle or surgical tissue biopsies.

Precision Radiotherapy

With any type of cancer, radiation therapy is effective at damaging and killing cancer cells. However, the treatment can also damage and kill surrounding healthy cells. Advances in imaging technologies are helping doctors to better target tumors and deliver

Proton Therapy

Proton therapy is a type of radiation treatment that can be used for adults and children with certain types of cancer. Compared to traditional X-ray radiation, proton therapy harms fewer of the healthy cells surrounding the cancer. In X-ray radiation, multiple X-ray beams aim at the cancer. The radiation focuses on the tumor, but some of it passes through the tumor and affects surrounding healthy cells. In comparison, proton radiation is more targeted. Doctors can make the radiation beam stop so that it does not pass through the tumor. This causes less damage to surrounding healthy cells. Proton therapy is most successful in treating solid cancer tumors that have not spread. It is commonly used to treat tumors in the brain, head, neck, lungs, and spine.

higher doses of radiation to cancer cells while sparing surrounding healthy cells.

At St. John's Hospital in Maplewood, Minnesota, a new technology allows doctors to perform precise radiation therapy and radiosurgery anywhere in the body. The system, called the Edge, allows doctors to deliver high doses of radiation to specific points, preventing damage to healthy cells and reducing treatment times significantly. "Being able to offer higher doses of radiation in fewer, faster treatments is a game changer," says Phil Silgen, a medical physicist at the hospital. "This technology has improved

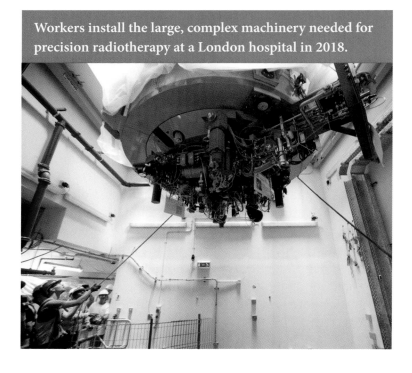

Workers install the large, complex machinery needed for precision radiotherapy at a London hospital in 2018.

the delivery, accuracy, and safety of radiation treatments for our patients, and opens the door for us to expand our radiosurgery capabilities to complex areas like the lungs and brain."[5]

> "Cancer treatments advance so much every single day and hope can be found in so many places."[6]
>
> —Clyde Lahnum, brain cancer survivor

Being diagnosed with cancer is one of the biggest health challenges a person can face in his or her lifetime. Cancer is a serious disease, and treatment often causes side effects that can last for weeks, months, and even years. Yet advances in science and medicine are improving outcomes for patients with cancer every day. More and more people are able to handle their cancer and go on to live healthy and productive lives.

Cancer Deaths Declining

Over the past 25 years, advances in cancer treatment, early detection, and prevention have caused the death rate from cancer to drop in the United States. According to statistics from the American Cancer Society reported in 2019, the cancer death rate declined steadily between 1991 and 2016. The combined cancer death rate for men and women fell 27 percent during that time.[7]

Essential
Facts

Facts about Cancer

- Approximately 1.8 million people were diagnosed with cancer in the United States in 2019.
- Approximately 607,000 people died of cancer in 2019 in the United States.
- Cancer occurs when cells in the body begin to divide abnormally and out of control.
- Cancer can develop in any part of the body.
- Risk factors such as age, chronic health conditions, family history, and exposure to harmful chemicals can increase the risk of developing cancers.
- Lifestyle choices such as smoking, drinking more than one to two alcoholic drinks daily, getting frequent exposure to the sun, and practicing unsafe sex can increase the risk of developing certain cancers.
- There is no guaranteed way to prevent cancer.

How Cancer Affects Daily Life

- A person going through cancer treatment may experience several physical effects, including pain, fatigue, lethargy, nausea, vomiting, and loss of appetite.
- Cancer and its treatment can cause a person's appearance to change. He or she may lose hair, gain or lose weight, or have skin problems. Surgery can cause scarring.
- Cancer diagnosis and treatment can trigger a flood of intense emotions.
- Patients may experience quickly changing moods and may struggle with anxiety and depression.

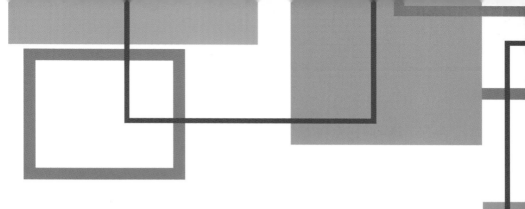

How Cancer Can Be Treated

- Common cancer treatments include surgery, radiation therapy, and chemotherapy.
- Most cancer treatments have side effects. These can include hair loss, mouth sores, nausea, vomiting, diarrhea, dry mouth, loss of appetite, skin rashes, swelling, fatigue, and changes in sleep patterns.
- Many cancer patients rely on a support network for physical, emotional, and financial help during and after treatment. A patient's support network may include family, friends, therapists, and support groups.
- Some cancer survivors experience delayed effects from treatment that emerge years after treatment ends.

Quote

"After my diagnosis, I felt like I had gone to a place none of my friends had been to before and no matter how hard I tried to describe it and how willing they were to try to understand, it was still an isolating experience. Meeting other young adult cancer patients and survivors gave me the validation that I am not the only person who has felt the way that I did. There are few things that have brought me as much comfort as hearing someone say, 'that happened to you too!?'"

—Gailon, a patient diagnosed with small round blue cell undifferentiated sarcoma

Glossary

amputation

The action of surgically cutting off a limb.

biopsy

The examination of tissue removed from a living patient to look for evidence of disease.

diagnosis

The identification of an illness in a person by a medical professional.

DNA

Deoxyribonucleic acid, the chemical that is the basis of genetics, through which various traits are passed from parent to child.

fatigue

Extreme tiredness.

hair follicle

The sheath of cells and connective tissue that surrounds the root of a hair.

inpatient

Having to do with a type of treatment where patients stay in a health-care facility.

intravenous (IV)

Happening within or entering through a vein.

lethargy

A lack of energy.

mutation

A change in a cell's genetic code.

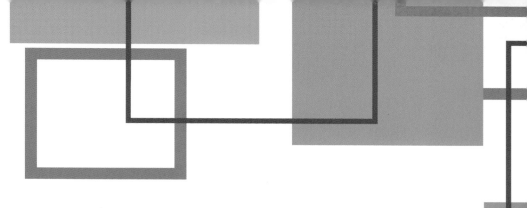

oncology

The study and treatment of cancer.

outpatient

Having to do with a type of treatment where patients do not need to stay in a health-care facility.

platelet

A disk-shaped cell found in the blood that is involved in clotting.

prognosis

A prediction of how a disease will turn out, including expected severity of symptoms, duration of illness, and sometimes chances of death.

secondhand smoke

Smoke given off when someone uses a tobacco product, which may be inhaled by someone other than the smoker.

sedate

To make a person or animal sleep by administering a drug.

transfusion

The act of transferring blood or similar products from one person or animal to another.

Additional
Resources

Selected Bibliography

"Facts & Figures 2019: US Cancer Death Rate Has Dropped 27% in 25 Years." *American Cancer Society*, 8 Jan. 2019, cancer.org. Accessed 24 Apr. 2020.

"Interview with Dr. Robert Goldsby: Beating Pediatric Cancer and Living Well." *UCSF Benioff Children's Hospital*, n.d., ucsfbenioffchildrens.org. Accessed 24 Apr. 2020.

Olsen, Karen. "Experts Forecast Cancer Research and Treatment Advances in 2020." *American Association for Cancer Research*, 10 Jan. 2020, aacr.org. Accessed 24 Apr. 2020.

"What Is Cancer?" *National Cancer Institute*, n.d., cancer.gov. Accessed 24 Apr. 2020.

Further Readings

Allman, Toney. *Kids and Cancer*. ReferencePoint, 2019.

Jackson, Vicki A., David P. Ryan, and Michelle D. Seaton. *Living with Cancer: A Step-by-Step Guide to Coping Medically and Emotionally with a Serious Diagnosis*. Johns Hopkins UP, 2017.

Morris, Alexandra. *Medical Research and Technology*. Abdo, 2016.

Online Resources

To learn more about handling cancer, please visit **abdobooklinks.com** or scan this QR code. These links are routinely monitored and updated to provide the most current information available.

More Information

For more information on this subject, contact or visit the following organizations:

American Cancer Society

250 Williams St. NW
Atlanta, GA 30303
800-227-2345
cancer.org
The American Cancer Society is a nonprofit community health organization that works to fight cancer.

American Childhood Cancer Organization

P.O. Box 498
Kensington, MD 20895
855-858-2226
acco.org
Founded in 1970, the American Childhood Cancer Organization is the country's oldest and largest organization dedicated to childhood cancer.

Source Notes

CHAPTER 1. LIVING WITH CANCER

1. "Acute Lymphoblastic Leukemia (ALL)." *St. Jude Children's Research Hospital*, 2020, stjude.org. Accessed 8 July 2020.

2. "In His Own Words: Living with Leukemia." *Winchester Hospital*, 2020, winchesterhospital.org. Accessed 8 July 2020.

3. Rebecca L. Siegel, Kimberly D. Miller, and Ahmedin Jemal. "Cancer Statistics, 2019." *CA: A Cancer Journal for Clinicians*, Jan. 2019, acsjournals.onlinelibrary.wiley.com. Accessed 8 July 2020.

4. Stacy Simon. "Facts & Figures 2019: US Cancer Death Rate Has Dropped 27% in 25 Years." *American Cancer Society*, 8 Jan. 2019, cancer.org. Accessed 17 July 2020.

5. "Victor's Story: Facing Each New Day with Gratitude." *This Is Living with Cancer*, June 2020, thisislivingwithcancer.com. Accessed 8 July 2020.

6. Siegel, Miller, and Jemal, "Cancer Statistics, 2019."

CHAPTER 2. WHAT IS CANCER?

1. "I Didn't Know What I Needed." *Teen Cancer America*, 4 Apr. 2018, teencanceramerica.org. Accessed 8 July 2020.

2. "Family Cancer Syndromes." *American Cancer Society*, 4 Jan. 2018, cancer.org. Accessed 8 July 2020.

3. "Outpacing Cancer with Exercise: An Interview with U of T's Linda Trinh." University of Toronto, 25 Oct. 2019, utoronto.ca. Accessed 6 Aug. 2020.

CHAPTER 3. DIAGNOSING CANCER

1. "In His Own Words: Living with Leukemia." *Winchester Hospital*, 2020, winchesterhospital.org. Accessed 8 July 2020.

2. "Ian McLoughlin." *Teen Cancer America*, 5 Jan. 2018, teencanceramerica.org. Accessed 8 July 2020.

3. "Brianna Talks Bridge Pose." *Teen Cancer America*, 1 Nov. 2016, teencanceramerica.org. Accessed 8 July 2020.

CHAPTER 4. GETTING TREATMENT

1. Rebecca Blomgren. "You Don't Have to Apologize for Your Feelings: It's Okay to Have a Meltdown." *Conquer*, Aug. 2019, conquer-magazine.com. Accessed 8 July 2020.

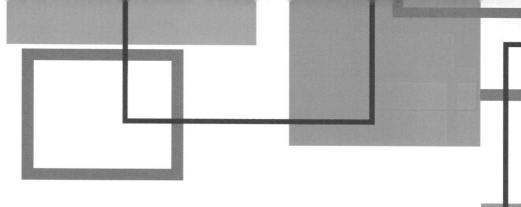

2. Blomgren, "You Don't Have to Apologize."

3. "Alec's Story for AYA Week." *Teen Cancer America*, 4 Apr. 2018, teencanceramerica.org. Accessed 8 July 2020.

4. Mia Brister. "First Love Yourself: Picking Up the Pieces." *Conquer*, Feb. 2020, conquer-magazine.com. Accessed 8 July 2020.

5. Ruth Wawszczyk. "A Teenager's Experience of Cancer." *Journal of the Royal Society of Medicine*, Aug. 2005, ncbi.nlm.nih.gov. Accessed 8 July 2020.

6. "The Emotional Aftermath of Cancer." *Roswell Park*, 9 May 2017, roswellpark.org. Accessed 8 July 2020.

CHAPTER 5. FINDING SUPPORT

1. "In His Own Words: Living with Leukemia." *Winchester Hospital*, 2020, winchesterhospital.org. Accessed 8 July 2020.

2. "Allison's Story: Fearless." *Children's Cancer Research Fund*, 16 Sept. 2019, childrenscancer.org. Accessed 8 July 2020.

3. "Elizabeth's Story – Fight with Ewing Sarcoma." *Children's Cancer Research Fund*, 26 Aug. 2019, childrenscancer.org. Accessed 8 July 2020.

4. "Friendships Lost and Found: Going Public with Cancer." *Roswell Park*, 25 Oct. 2016, roswellpark.org. Accessed 8 July 2020.

5. "Finding Support Systems for People with Cancer." *National Comprehensive Cancer Network*, 2020, nccn.org. Accessed 8 July 2020.

6. "TCA Advocate Discusses Sarcoma Awareness Month." *Teen Cancer America*, 11 July 2019, teencanceramerica.org. Accessed 8 July 2020.

7. "Finding Support Systems for People with Cancer."

8. "In His Own Words: Living with Leukemia."

9. "Alyssa Reflects on Life During AYA Week." *Teen Cancer America*, 6 Apr. 2018, teencanceramerica.org. Accessed 8 July 2020.

Source Notes
Continued

CHAPTER 6. HOW CANCER AFFECTS DAILY LIFE

1. "Meet 11-Year-Old Ella: Tree of Hope 2019 Tree Lighter." *Roswell Park*, 9 Dec. 2019, roswellpark.org. Accessed 8 July 2020.

2. Rebecca Blomgren. "You Don't Have to Apologize for Your Feelings: It's Okay to Have a Meltdown." *Conquer*, Aug. 2019, conquer-magazine.com. Accessed 8 July 2020.

3. Patrick Eck. "From Teen to Survivor: Living with the Effects of Cancer Years Later." *Cancer.Net*, 2 Apr. 2019, cancer.net. Accessed 8 July 2020.

4. "I'm Happy, and I Am Alive." *Roswell Park*, 30 Dec. 2016, roswellpark.org. Accessed 8 July 2020.

5. "Keep Up with Your Daily Routine." *National Cancer Institute*, 24 Jan. 2019, cancer.gov. Accessed 8 July 2020.

CHAPTER 7. CANCER AND SCHOOL

1. "Rates of Children and Teens Getting Cancer by State or Region." *Centers for Disease Control and Prevention*, 1 Oct. 2018, cdc.gov. Accessed 8 July 2020.

2. "Allison: Bone Cancer Survivor." *Yale Cancer Center*, 24 Sept. 2019, yalecancercenter.org. Accessed 8 July 2020.

3. "Jordan Finds His Way." *Teen Cancer America*, 12 Oct. 2016, teencanceramerica.org. Accessed 8 July 2020.

4. "Alyssa Reflects on Life During AYA Week." *Teen Cancer America*, 6 Apr. 2018, teencanceramerica.org. Accessed 8 July 2020.

5. "Lily's Story." *Kids Cancer Care*, 23 July 2019, kidscancercare.ab.ca. Accessed 8 July 2020.

6. "Going Back to School." *13thirty*, n.d., 13thirty.org. Accessed 8 July 2020.

CHAPTER 8. LIVING AS A SURVIVOR

1. "Cancer Statistics." *National Cancer Institute*, 27 Apr. 2018, cancer.gov. Accessed 8 July 2020.

2. "Cancer Statistics."

3. Maya Harsaniova. "The Power of Here and Now." *Conquer*, Feb. 2019, conquer-magazine.com. Accessed 8 July 2020.

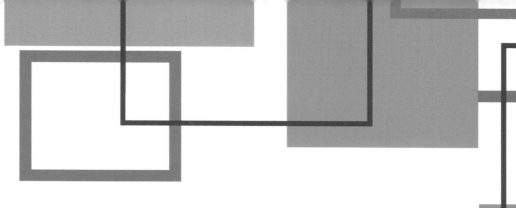

4. "Life after Cancer." *American Cancer Society*, 2020, cancer.org. Accessed 8 July 2020.

5. "Having Cancer as a Teenager Derailed My Life." *Teen Cancer America*, 11 Sept. 2019, teencanceramerica.org. Accessed 8 July 2020.

6. "Interview with Dr. Robert Goldsby: Beating Pediatric Cancer and Living Well." *UCSF Benioff Children's Hospital*, 2019, ucsfbenioffchildrens.org. Accessed 8 July 2020.

7. "Cancer Gave Me a Cause." *Teen Cancer America*, 6 Apr. 2018, teencanceramerica.org. Accessed 8 July 2020.

CHAPTER 9. TREATMENT EVOLVES

1. "A Diagnosis of Cancer Doesn't Have to Be a Death Sentence Now." *Bayer Scientific Magazine*, 9 Oct. 2017, research.bayer.com. Accessed 8 July 2020.

2. Karen Olsen. "Experts Forecast Cancer Research and Treatment Advances in 2020." *American Association for Cancer Research*, 10 Jan. 2020, aacr.org. Accessed 8 July 2020.

3. Olsen, "Experts Forecast Cancer Research in 2020."

4. "CAR T Cells: Engineering Patients' Immune Cells to Treat Their Cancers." *National Cancer Institute*, 30 July 2019, cancer.gov. Accessed 8 July 2020.

5. "St. John's Unveils New Cutting-Edge Cancer Treatment Technology." *Fairview*, 31 Oct. 2018, fairview.org. Accessed 8 July 2020.

6. Clyde Lahnum. "Clyde's Story: Surviving a Cancerous Brain Tumor." *Roswell Park*, 2 Oct. 2017, roswellpark.org. Accessed 8 July 2020.

7. Stacy Simon. "Facts & Figures 2019: US Cancer Death Rate Has Dropped 27% in 25 Years." *American Cancer Society*, 8 Jan. 2019, cancer.org. Accessed 8 July 2020.

Index

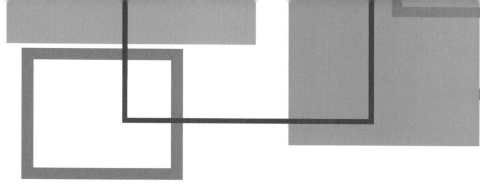

About the
Author

Carla Mooney

Carla Mooney is the author of many books for young adults and children. She lives in Pittsburgh, Pennsylvania, with her husband and three children.

About the Consultant
Dr. Christopher Donnelly

Dr. Christopher Donnelly is a board-certified dentist and a PhD-trained scientist at Duke University with scientific expertise in cancer immunology and neuroscience. Clinically, Dr. Donnelly's focus is on patients suffering from complex issues involving the head and neck. He has published many original research articles on the biological mechanisms that regulate cancer progression, cancer metastasis, and cancer-associated pain, work which has led him to receive several research accolades and awards. After the diagnosis of a parent with advanced-stage cancer several years ago, Dr. Donnelly also experienced "the other side" of cancer, gaining an up close and personal familiarity with how the disease and its treatment affects an individual and loved ones. Dr. Donnelly lives in Durham, North Carolina, with his wife and their two dogs and cats.